CW00864874

Barefoot Christ

Why Barefoot Christ?

Where would the Barefoot Christ be found in the Global Village? Or where would He hang out?

The meaning of all things according to the Barefoot Christ or more importantly what is life all about?

What is the message of the Barefoot Christ in today's Global Village and its context?

Epilogue

Barefoot Christ

What if Christ walked amongst
us barefoot ?
Barefoot and full of humility and
as a servant.
Barefoot no sandals or shoes to
protect His feet.
Where would He go?

Would He walk barefoot
amongst the marginalized,
poor and dispossessed of our
world?
Would He walk in the Favella's
of Brazil or the shanty-towns of

Cape Town ?
Or would He walk in the
neighborhoods of Beverly Hills
or those of the ' rich and famous '?

The Barefoot Christ
The Son of God and the
Son of Man.
Full of Divinity, Grace and
Truth !

1. Why Barefoot Christ?

The question is why a book and ensuing discussion about the Barefoot Christ? For a long time I have understood we make or even sometimes re-make Jesus Christ in our particular cultural image? That can come with all our particular cultural baggage. What if we could strip the Son of God Jesus Christ back to who He was in reality? Which is why essentially write a book entitled Barefoot Christ.

What would it look like if Jesus Christ walked around Barefoot in our C21st Global Village proclaiming His message of the Kingdom of God. Barefoot because in our world even your shoes tell you so much about a person, who they are, what they believe in and of course their status in the Global Village. Shoes can tell you so much about a person and individual. Sometimes they can be all about pretending to be somebody or something we are not and can never be?

To further develop the idea if Christ was barefoot where would He go on this planet? One thing I would know He would be stepping into the very messes of our Global Village. Because His feet would simply have no protection against those very messes on the ground.

For me that is a picture of what Jesus Christ did 2,000 years ago. He entered our world in Galilee and He entered it knowing full well how messy and full of conflict that world really was in.   At times we can romantically believe that He does not know how messy the world and our very lives really are? The problem is that He does and yet in the face of it continues to love both us as individual's and the Global Village.

' For God so loved the world that He gave His only Son ....' That statement is true even in this day and age. For me it will always be a given, a very real truism that I can really anchor the way I both approach, engage and view the Global Village. The Father and His Son and the Holy Spirit still love the Global Village and that has not changed and it really can be and should be an anchor for our faith in the One true God.

Part of that love for the Global Village is that he made a way back to him through the death, burial and resurrection of His Son Jesus Christ. That is a gift that has been both an anchor and a means and vehicle of change and growth in my life. His message has not changed in 2,000 years along with the love of the Father shown through Him for the Global Village.

Stop and think about the very people you meet each day of your life and maybe just maybe in each face you see, you see a glimpse, just a glimpse of the Barefoot Christ? This is based on the premise that we are each made in the ' imago deo ', the image of God. I will grant you that image may well be corrupted by the Fall but something of it remains and is visible in each and every person we meet and engage with each day?

Sometimes in my lighter moments I can imagine that in a Christian person that Jesus Christ peeks out of the windows of their eyes and the blinds of their eyes are sometimes up. Interesting idea is it not Jesus Christ peeking out of somebody's eyes? Might make you scared maybe to look in a person's eyes and become aware of who maybe looking back through their gaze? It may well be the risen Son of God, the One who everything revolves around and is centered upon.

Sometimes I believe more and more we need to be prepared to take Jesus Christ on His terms rather than painting Him as the Christ our minds want to believe in? I guess I believe we need to believe in the unvarnished, unadulterated and definitely not politically - correct Jesus Christ the Son of God. Not the cardboard cut-out version we are sometimes sold by some ' religious types ' in the Global Village. The Man from Galilee still wants us to be in relationship with Him, the real Son of God, not the fictional one or the one of vain imagination? That relationship is what we offer as we share the message of Jesus Christ the Son of God.

There is a marvelous statue as statue's go I guess in Rio of Jesus Christ above the very city of Rio. The reason I want you to think about that statue of Jesus Christ is because it is a picture of the One I am calling the Barefoot Christ? The thing I love about that statue is that the very arms of the figure on the statue are open wide. Which shows me and reminds me in the form of a statue that Jesus Christ still to this day wants to embrace individual's and the Global Village. When we find ourselves in His embrace and he wraps His arms around us, we find life and real comfort and warmth. The embrace of the Man from Galilee, it really is joy unspeakable.

His embraces still this day people's lives in the Global Village. I hope and pray you long for and still long for the embrace of the Man from Galilee, the Barefoot Christ?

2. Where would the Barefoot Christ be found in the Global Village? Or where would He hang out?

I do not know whether you have ever thought about where would the Barefoot Christ be found in the Global Village of today? Or put more specifically where would the Barefoot Christ hand out, with whom would He hang out and where is He to be found in the Global Village?

Some may hate me for saying it but I would believe He would

be found amongst the poor, diseased and marginalized of the Global Village? He would still be hanging out where the so-called ' sinners ' of the Global Village hang out? His ' modes operandi ' has not changed, He still has compassion, care and love for the people who are overlooked and marginalized in the Global Village. So I would think He would be quite comfortable in villages or shanty - towns with houses and homes made out of cardboard and any material that comes to hand. Those of Cape Town South Africa and the favella's of Rio, Brazil? He would still be loving and walking with and amongst those who have no real economic power, status or even material wealth? He would be loving them in the midst of the very real messiness of their lives. I believe further that He would enter into that messiness and bring His presence and life into it. This perspective on where He would presence Himself is part and parcel why this book is called the Barefoot Christ?

Sometimes I/we can want to dictate who can come to Him and even at times where His presence, influence, power and authority should be shown and found? We/I need always to remember He really is the One who has all authority and power given to Him by His Father. The Global Village and its nation-states belong rightfully to Him and His Father. He does not have to win or even buy them back. He has the right of possession, they are His property as well as the people and people-groups in them. His ownership and His rights regards that are something we all need to wrestle with more and more?

   At times we/I can I believe even go as far as wanting to dictate who is in or who is out? To me there is a tendency to want to ' play God ' and literally sit in the throne occupied by ' Father God '. There is only ever going to be one true God and Godhead and as far as I know the job and jobs are filled? At times we can be ' control freaks ' and want to control everything in our world, worlds and even in our very lives. I guess in some ways what happens when we come to know the Man from Galilee is that we cede and give over to Him control of our very lives? The very control we think we exercise over our lives is very illusory and also mirage-like? We need to let God be God and not seek to exercise control over things we have no right to exercise, people, places and situations.

Sometimes culture and our very real cultural baggage can and does dictate and even determine our belief and our belief- systems regarding the Man from Galilee. The Global Village has now grown incredibly weary and worn out of the cut-out, clear eyed, blond haired, airbrushed and all together Westernized version of the Man from Galilee. We all need to shed our own cultural baggage and be prepared to engage with the Man from Galilee on His terms and the very real reality of Him. I guess as I grow older I tend not to believe the airbrushed, cut-out version of the Man from Galilee? Australians and the people of the Global Village want and are dying from thirst for the ' fair dinkum ' version of the Man from Galilee.

Sometimes sadly all people get from us is the airbrushed, cardboard cut-out version of the Man from Galilee. My real question for you and I is how can they grab hold of and accept someone who is not presented, revealed and shared with them correctly? There is a very real desire and thirst for the real, true and authentic Man from Galilee. It is almost like the question being asked is will the real Man from Galilee please stand up? We all need the real Man from Galilee to both stand up and be revealed, now more than ever. The politically correct, sanitized and message full of our cultural baggage do not cut it anymore. The real Man from Galilee, the Barefoot Christ needs to be shared, revealed and apprehended by the Global Village now more than ever. The Man from Galilee, the Barefoot Christ, the One who can and will bring about the change and real change we all want to see in the Global Village of our day.

3. The meaning of all things according to the Barefoot Christ or more importantly what is life all about?

At times we I believe can ' major on the minors and minor on the majors'. We can have a tendency to make life all about things that are really of no value in terms of the *kingdom of God.* Sometimes it can be all about us and our own little *kingdoms* rather than being all about His kingdom-and the worship of Him through our lives. At times we all can want to make it something it is really not?

My reflection upon my own life is that sometimes and may well be all the time I am really a bit actor or player who has a part to play in his-story but is not essential to either the end of his-story or even the end of the story. Self-importance and an inflated sense of our own value is and can be great for our self-esteem. But the question lies in how does that relate to the kingdom of God and His plans and purposes? To my own thinking it has and will always be Plan A in relation to the kingdom of God and that does not shift or change for me or anybody else who may claim to be part of His kingdom people? There really is no darkness or shadow-line in His kingdom or His plans for His kingdom to come and that is present in the here and now. He is like a mountain range called the Dividing range in NSW, Australia it does not bend, buckle, shift or move. ' His will done on earth as it is done in heaven.' So the Man from Galilee taught us to pray to His Father in the LORD'S prayer. Which is in so many ways reveals His heart and the very heart of His Father.

In relation to this you could think of the Barefoot Christ as being the Naked Christ? Particularly in relation to His kingdom and Plan A otherwise known as Salvation or Redemptive His-Story. He will get the Global Village to the point where it needs to be ' all things work together for good for those who love the LORD and are known by Him'.

The Westminster Confession which is a wonderful confession

of truth about the one true-God, His character and what He requires. I think the first statement sums up what the Barefoot Christ requires of us as His people. ' The chief end of man is to worship God '. If you ever wondered what your chief end goal and purpose was in life; it is to worship God.

Before you double-take and think I mean by worship singing a few choruses on Sunday Church in the morning service? Once there was a gentleman who lectured me in theology. He defined worship of God in terms of everything in your life being able to be seen as worship to God. If everything you do in your life could be and can be worship to and of God everything can be viewed in much different ways?

I have found my friend's definition of what worship of God looks like incredibly helpful in my lief and walking out my discipleship of the Man from Galilee and Him as the Barefoot Christ? Further I would believe this definition of worship accords very well with the picture of worship of God the Word of God itself paints in it. The one true God wants us to worship in both ' spirit and truth ' [John 4] and also with everything in and through our lives.

The subtext of the heading of this chapter is what life is all about in relation to the Barefoot Christ and being in relationship with Him in the C21st Global Village? The above statements about all of our lives being worship are my response to that question. As the Westminster Confession does say the chief end of man is to worship God and that i believe or would propose is what life is all about in the end? Further I would believe that when everything in our lives is about that; then we are fulfilled in terms of the purpose and destiny of our lives as well. Everybody today talks about self-fulfillment of oneself but what if its all about the chief end of life being the worship of the God who is other than ourselves? The one true God who is other and outside and beyond time and space and the One who is truly eternally God? So in the end when all our lives are worship to the one true God, the Father, the Son and the Holy Spirit. We become everything we were always meant to be.

To further develop this argument I would understand that everybody in the Global Village has a theology? There is a world-view , or belief or ideology that both inspires and drives all their actions and practices in their everyday lives. Even the so-called atheists have a theology that drives their lives. Despite their apparent non-belief in God it does drive their lives and outworks itself as their theology in practice. The difference between them and people of the Christian faith community is that our very faith and belief in the one true God drives us to Him with all of our lives. The problem or dilemma everybody faces is that it is not ever acceptable to be half-hearted or even half-baked regards this worship or its practice in your life regards Him. For a long time I have imagined the picture of life as being one where you can do some fishing on one side or the other but there are definitely ' no-fence-sitters ' allowed. To add to it further there really is no fence in the middle that exists in reality with regards to who and what you worship with all your life. This is particularly true in the Global Village of today.

The interesting thing in the Global Village is that people of any faith, even the Christian faith are viewed as being naive and even as dangerous? The problem I have is that it is not easy to walk in the footsteps of the Barefoot Christ? As He did say ' if anyone wants to follow me let him take up his cross and follow me'. The interesting aspect of that is when we seek to do it the Barefoot Christ walks it out with us in real life. Unlike ' footsteps ' I would believe that the Barefoot Christ sometimes and may well be all the time walks beside us rather than just carrying us when times are hard in our lives?

The Barefoot Christ , the One with no illusions, no pretensions or biases walks beside us throughout our very lives in the Global Village. That is what He has done with the children of His Father for the last 2,000 years of the his-story of the Global Village. He has and does literally walk with His Father's children. The Barefoot Christ is therefore very much present and a present reality with the children of His Father.

As you can probably imagine

there is and should be tremendous security and warmth in that very reality of Him walking with us? He still does that with this child and He does that as the Barefoot Christ .... Amen.

4.What is the message of the Barefoot Christ in today's Global Village and its context?

Sometimes we can get mixed messages even from those of the Barefoot Christ even just from the Christ. At times we do not deal with the message of the Barefoot Christ because to do so would be incredibly confronting for us? At times we/I want to make the Barefoot Christ politically correct, make it the sanitized and easily digestible version of His message? I have come, more and more to the belief that we need to deal with His message on His terms and its terms. To not do so is to impose something foreign to it and His message?

The message of the Barefoot Christ will always be, has always been and will for evermore incredibly confronting and even dare I say offensive to some. The message of the Barefoot Christ demands everything from us, no half-halfheartedness. Total commitment to Him, His cause and His message. All of which is not by its very nature popular in today's Global Village. Total commitment in terms of your life being worship to the One known as the Barefoot Christ is not very popular fodder for the masses. Therefore what some parts of the Body of the Barefoot Christ have done is dumb-down both the commitment required of both. The very real cost of walking in His footsteps in the messiness of the Global Village today is commitment to Him but His message. Sometimes that has and can be portrayed,marketed and sold as wanting to be culturally appropriate to the Global Village?

It can be and usually is hard to walk in and out of the footsteps of the Barefoot Christ in today's Global Village. As i have noted earlier ' faith '; any form of ' faith ' in a ' god ' is not very popular or even politically correct?

To develop the concept of the Barefoot Christ and His message for the Global Village of today; think about the idea of being barefoot? The Barefoot Christ's message when it comes from the Barefoot Christ consists of the faith of a child. Not a faith that is childish faith but rather faith consisting of both the trust, belief and openness of a child. As he is known to have said ' we cannot enter the kingdom of God unless we come as a child '. To come as a child to the Barefoot Christ also means and involves having no illusions or pretensions about your position before and in relation to the Barefoot Christ. We come to barefoot, naked and child – like to the Barefoot Christ. Trusting in His love, care and compassion for us in our nakedness, humility and honesty. For me that is how we all need to come before and to the Barefoot Christ. It is the point He, His Father and the Holy Spirit are always trying to bring us to in our lives. To be honest sometimes one has to hit ' rock bottom ' before one can come to the Barefoot Christ, His Father and the Holy Spirit. It is almost like the basic requirement the Barefoot Christ and the Godhead have for coming into relationship with them? The Barefoot Christ wants and really demands everything from us when He calls us into relationship with Him as the Barefoot Christ.

To not come as a child, with child - like faith, humility and openness does not work with the Barefoot Christ.

The Barefoot Christ was, is and always will be; the way, the truth and the life. There is no other way to come to the Father but through Him and as a child. I would admit and acknowledge to come to the Barefoot Christ will and can mean our pride, ourselves and our desires and wants need to be crushed and bow their knees to Him. Yet the truth is that when this happens to us, He heals, tends and even mends our brokenness and makes us whole in Him. I do not know of any other way to be made whole or to be in the process of being made whole than coming to walk with the Barefoot Christ?

Another aspect of coming as a child to the Barefoot Christ in today's

Global Village. Is that children of all races, colors and creeds are very quick to forgive each other when they hurt each other?

Think deeply; very deeply for some of us, about what happens with children at your local school and how the playground and its various battles works? Children do hurt, hate each other at times and also wound each other. Yet the same children; particularly when they are still children are known to be very forgiving in their battles, wars and conflicts with each other in their playgrounds? In this very real forgiveness the children of the school playground have much to teach us so –

called adults of the Global village of today?

In some way maybe that is simply why the hope for the future of the Global Village; does in reality lie with the forgiveness of the children of the multitude of playgrounds throughout the Global Village. Sometimes when we grow-up too much and unlearn the very real - art - of - forgiveness we all learn in our playgrounds we have left behind too much of our childhood's. Now more than ever the message of the Barefoot Christ would be that we all need to come as a child. But also that we all need to relearn the lessons of our playgrounds regarding the wondrous art of forgiving each other much.

The Global Village needs to see and learn and perhaps relearn the art of the forgiveness of the playground? In so many ways so much of our shared future for our common humanity depends on us relearning these arts and processes again? I know the Global Village is not a child's playground but sometimes the picture and images of it are not too far removed from that of the playground? May well be that is why the Barefoot Christ when he was on the earth loved children coming and spending time with Him? Also why we need to come to Him as the Barefoot Christ in the very reality of a child?

There have been times usually in my darker moments when I believe we all should put the children of the Global Village in charge of both the UN and our own nation-states? Mainly because I would propose the children of the Global Village might when all is said and done do a great job of running both? So that may well be our future and that is something we will have to wait and see if it unfolds that way?

This could be important in terms of us all dealing with the future? Because the children of the Global Village seem sometimes to have lost their faith and belief in the adults of the Global Village. The age-old question we all have before us in the Village is how does one restore the faith in and belief of the children of the Global Village?

The message of the Barefoot Christ is needed all the more in these days and at this hour in the his-story of the Global Village. His message may by its nature be in and of itself offensive to some but the hunger, thirst and desires of many in the Global Village is crying out for it. The lessons of the playground's of our youth may well have to be rediscovered and relearned. In particular the lessons of being quick to forgive others?

Epilogue :

The Barefoot Christ still beckons us to come, rest with Him awhile and walk through the highways and cities of the Global Village. The Barefoot Christ is not bound up in our very real pretensions and even assumptions about Him. He continues to and does show up in some very funny places and interesting places throughout the Global Village to this very day. He is not politically correct and His barefoot message can and still is as offensive to many ears as it was during His time on the earth.

Sometimes and may well

be all the time we need as his followers to be prepared to walk with Him barefoot and as a child in the Global Village. When we seek to walk with Him barefoot, naked and as a child He can, does and will use us in some very profound ways. The Barefoot Christ is still very much present, alive and existing in the Global Village of today.

As was noted there is a real desire, hunger and thirst I believe for the Barefoot Christ; the one of the Word of God. The Barefoot Christ is the One who can bring the change and life we all want to see in our days and times. There can be and always is hope to be found in the life and ministry in the Global Village of the Barefoot Christ. So I would encourage you to go and be prepared in your life to go barefoot with the Barefoot Christ in today's Global Village ....

Shalom and Amen and Amen.

Lightning Source UK Ltd.
Milton Keynes UK
UKRC011814120619
344204UK00009B/237

* 9 7 8 1 3 6 7 3 3 8 6 1 6 *